D1523696

# JOBS IN THE
# U.S. NAVY

ERIC NDIKUMANA

ROSEN
PUBLISHING

New York

Published in 2023 by The Rosen Publishing Group, Inc.
29 East 21st Street, New York, NY 10010

First Edition

Portions of this work were originally authored by Taylor Baldwin Kiland and published as *Careers in the U.S. Navy*. All new material in this edition was authored by Eric Ndikumana.

Library of Congress Cataloging-in-Publication Data

Names: Ndikumana, Eric, author.
Title: Jobs in the U.S. Navy / Eric Ndikumana.
Description: New York : Rosen Publishing, [2023] | Series: Exploring
    military careers | Includes bibliographical references and index.
Identifiers: LCCN 2021057473 (print) | LCCN 2021057474 (ebook) | ISBN
    9781499470024 (library binding) | ISBN 9781499470017 (paperback) | ISBN
    9781499470031 (ebook)
Subjects: LCSH: United States. Navy—Vocational guidance—Juvenile
    literature | United States. Navy—Juvenile literature
Classification: LCC VB259 .N35 2023  (print) | LCC VB259  (ebook) | DDC
    359.002373—dc23/eng/20211209
LC record available at https://lccn.loc.gov/2021057473
LC ebook record available at https://lccn.loc.gov/2021057474

Some of the images in this book illustrate individuals who are models. The depictions do not imply actual situations or events.

*Manufactured in the United States of America*

CPSIA Compliance Information: Batch #CSRYA23. For further information, contact Rosen Publishing, New York, New York, at 1-800-237-9932.

Find us on

# CONTENTS

# CHAPTER 1

# DEFINING THE NAVY

**W**hen European travelers first began colonizing North America, their settlements were close to the coast. Easy access to the sea helped coastal cities, including New York and Boston, become international trading centers. Though the United States has nearly 3,000 miles (4,828 km) of land between its east and west coasts, nearly half of all Americans still live in counties on the coast. For all these reasons—and more—it has always been important that the United States have a naval force that could defend its waters.

Originally founded in 1775 to fight against the British, the U.S. Navy has grown to be a worldwide peacekeeping force. Naval ships protect trade routes all around the globe, ensuring that commercial vessels can sail safely without fear of attack. As a military force, it can also be rapidly deployed to protect U.S. interests anywhere in the world.

The turn of the 21st century brought about major changes to international conflicts, and the navy—just like every armed service branch—has had to adapt to this new breed of warfare. Following the September 11 attacks, ships of the navy were increasingly assigned to missions involving the interception and disruption of terrorist activities around the world. With massive ships and advanced technology, the navy is perfectly suited to accomplishing these missions while also supporting ground and air troops as they are deployed to fight the nation's enemies.

## HUMBLE BEGINNINGS

Before it became a global fighting force, the navy was established to help the new United States fight off the British. For many years, European naval powers—the Spanish, Portuguese, British, and Dutch, among others—had made their empires nearly unstoppable. Full-scale sea battles were common, and the nations with the most advanced ships and best sailors became feared across the globe.

In the 1770s, the American colonies did not have a unified seafaring force. Volunteers who fought

Before the rise of new ship technology in the 1800s, the nation with the best wooden navy was often the most powerful.

against the British sometimes had sailing experience, but most were merchants who had seen little actual fighting. In 1775, following heated debate, it was determined that the new nation needed to be able to defend its coast if it were ever going to be free, and the Continental Navy was established.

Supported by ships from France, the young navy produced solid results during the Revolutionary War. Knowing that their vessels could never compete with the British fleet in open fighting, American captains instead tried to pull their enemies into smaller engagements. Some naval actions even took place far from American soil, such as the Battle of

Flamborough Head, which took place in 1779 off the coast of northern England. In this dramatic battle, Captain John Paul Jones, commander of the *Bonhomme Richard*, successfully fought off two British ships and disrupted the trading convoy those ships were protecting. Though Flamborough Head involved fewer than 10 ships, more than 250 sailors died in the battle.

The Battle of Flamborough Head was one of the earliest victories for U.S. naval forces.

Despite the terrible death toll, Jones's victory confirmed his heroic reputation and earned him a personal place in history as the "Father of the American Navy." The battle also cemented a new, winning reputation for the nation's young navy. This newfound respect was critical, for the United States would come to have more enemies than just the British in the years to come.

# SHIP BATTLE BRAVERY

The history of the U.S. Navy is full of heroic sailors who went above and beyond the call of duty. One early ship battle hero was William Hamilton, a sailor aboard the *Bonhomme Richard*. Going into battle against the HMS *Serapis*, Hamilton understood that the enemy had superior firepower—but he also knew that Commodore Jones was wearing down the enemy's ability to fight because he refused to give up. In the midst of fighting, while the two ships were entangled, Hamilton seized an opportunity to deliver the final blow. He climbed out onto the yardarm with a basket of hand grenades and a live match, lit the fuse, and dropped a grenade right into an open hatch of the *Serapis*. It landed on some gunpowder that had been left unprotected. The explosions and fire that erupted killed more than 20 enemy men and seriously wounded many others. Exhausted from heated battle against a stubborn opponent—and disheartened by Hamilton's courageous assault—the captain of the *Serapis* finally surrendered to Jones, securing a victory for the navy.

# PIRACY TROUBLES

Sailing the Mediterranean in the early 1800s, pirate groups were loosely organized and never officially working for any particular government. They were causing physical damage to the ships they attacked, harming sailors, and stealing valuable goods intended for the free market. To protect merchant ships throughout the world, the United States once again launched into war.

After gaining independence from Britain, the United States could not afford to keep the Continental Navy active, so Congress got rid of all the American warships. Soon after, when American merchants attempted to travel the globe for trading purposes, they encountered a new kind of threat. Patrolling the Mediterranean Sea mostly unchecked, bands of pirates were not looking to control land or people; they were looking for money. They freely attacked American merchant ships that traveled by the Barbary States: Algiers, Tunis, Morocco, and Tripoli. They demanded payment, or else they would take the crew and ship hostage—until a ransom was paid.

One of those ships was the USS *Philadelphia*, which ran aground and was captured in the Tripoli harbor along with her crew in 1803. Early negotiations were unsuccessful, and the *Philadelphia* remained hostage thousands of miles from home.

Lieutenant Stephen Decatur was a young naval officer, but he came up with a daring plan. Decatur decided to disguise a recently captured ship, the

USS *Intrepid*, as a friendly vessel and sneak up for a surprise attack. In February 1804, Decatur and his crew quietly sailed into the Tripoli harbor and came up to the *Philadelphia*. His crew asked for an anchor line in Arabic—the local language—pretending that the *Intrepid* had lost its own. At close range, the pirates recognized the foreigners and alerted the rest of the crew, but Decatur and his small band were still able to board the *Philadelphia*.

After a short period of brutal hand-to-hand fighting, the Americans overpowered the Tripolitans. With the pirates defeated and the *Philadelphia*'s crew saved, Decatur set the *Philadelphia* ablaze and—just as quickly as they arrived—the Americans jumped back with rescued sailors onto the *Intrepid*. They slid out of the harbor as the *Philadelphia* burned to the waterline. Called the Battle of Tripoli, the surprise attack embarrassed the enemy while proving the navy's ability—once again—to do more than just defend the American coastline.

## FIGHTING THE BRITISH—AGAIN

Though the United States had won its independence, it did not take long for the British to seek control over its former colonies again. In the early 1800s, during its ongoing struggle for power in the world, Great Britain was taking notice of the United States' increase in international trade. The United States' economy more than doubled between 1795 and 1806.

Lieutenant Stephen Decatur was the clever young naval officer who came up with the battle plan that led to a U.S. victory in the Battle of Tripoli.

The British started by imposing tariffs—or taxes—on the goods the United States attempted to ship through British ports. Not long after, British ships began to appear along the eastern U.S. seaboard, taunting American merchant ships. By then, President James Madison was fed up, and he asked Congress for a declaration of war against the British on June 1, 1812.

Americans did not sit back and rest after winning their first war against the British. Off the coast of Nova Scotia in 1812 sat a shining example of American skill in shipbuilding: the USS *Constitution*. Its sides were reinforced with metal, making them hard to penetrate by weapons of the day. In mid-August 1812, a lookout noticed a British ship on the horizon. Isaac Hull, the *Constitution*'s captain, immediately recognized the HMS *Guerrière*, since he knew James Dacres, its captain. Dacres believed his ship was faster in the water than the *Constitution*, and he mistakenly thought that this would ensure his victory. When the battle between the ships began, however, the *Constitution* was skillfully maneuvered to dance around the *Guerrière*. When the British cannon shots did hit the *Constitution*, they appeared to bounce off the hull, earning the ship the nickname "Old Ironsides." In the meantime, the *Constitution* struck the *Guerrière* repeatedly with devastating fire and was able to break the mizzenmast of the *Guerrière* with a few well-placed broadsides, completely disabling the ship. Dacres surrendered.

The War of 1812 ushered in a new era for the U.S. Navy, and the USS *Constitution* was a major part in the nation's increasing naval power.

This victory encouraged the Americans, who were suffering significant defeats in land battles during the War of 1812. It also shocked the British at home, as they were confident that their naval superiority was assured. It turned out that there was a new naval player on the world stage: the United States.

## FIGHTING UP NORTH

During the War of 1812, the border between the United States and Canada became a battlefield. In fact, some Americans who supported this second conflict with the British were intent on also conquering Canada. During the war, land and naval forces were sent to the Great Lakes region to mount invasions against the northern neighbors.

Master Commandant Oliver Hazard Perry took command of the American naval forces in Lake Erie in the spring of 1813 and quickly assembled a squadron of more than 10 vessels, outfitting these ships with sharpshooters borrowed from the U.S. Army. He staged his fleet in the western end of Lake Erie, antagonizing the British fleet and disrupting its control of the lake.

With his supply lines in jeopardy, the British naval commander Captain Robert H. Barclay had no choice but to engage Perry—despite being severely outmatched in firepower. The two fleets met in September 1813. Perry's flagship, the USS *Lawrence*, took the lead and attacked the British at a shallow angle to minimize the effect of the British gunfire.

Master Commandant Perry was a heroic figure during the War of 1812, and his tactical prowess became well respected.

However, the USS *Lawrence*'s early advantage turned into a disadvantage, as the rest of Perry's squadron took too long to catch up. The USS *Lawrence* took most of the casualties, with 80 percent of the crew killed or wounded. Recognizing that the *Lawrence* was failing, Perry and a small crew rowed over to another ship—the USS *Niagara*—to continue the battle. Perry maneuvered the USS *Niagara* across the bows of two of the British ships engaged with

Perry is shown here leading a small crew as they sail to the *Niagara* after abandoning the damaged *Lawrence*.

the USS *Lawrence*, ordered the remaining vessels in his fleet to back him up, and engaged the tired British from the front, forcing them to surrender. With victory at hand, Perry wrote a quick note to his superiors, marking a turning point in the war.

While this battle and other battles in the Great Lakes were not full-scale naval engagements, they were some of the fiercest battles of the entire war. More important than their size was their impact on the eventual outcome of the conflict: American naval victories in the Great Lakes forced the British to give up their invasion of Ohio and allowed the U.S. Army to take the offensive.

The War of 1812 was relatively short—ending with a peace treaty signed in 1814—but it saw both sides gain advantages over its course. Repeatedly beaten back by the U.S. Navy, Britain found itself unable to take control of the Great Lakes region, slowing their advance. The Americans were quick to seize their opportunities, but those who wanted the United States to conquer Canada were left disappointed. Though there was no clear winner in the War of 1812, the U.S. Navy once more proved that it was worthy of global respect.

# CHAPTER 2

# THE EARLY DAYS OF THE NAVY

Life as a young nation is not easy. In its first century of independence from Britain, the United States faced many struggles. One of the biggest and trickiest was what to do with the economy, especially as the country kept expanding with the annexation of new states. The darkest stain in U.S. history is the slave trade, and in the 1850s, most southern states relied on slave labor to drive their agricultural economy. As cries for abolition grew louder—and Abraham Lincoln was elected president—most southern states left the Union to form the Confederate States of America, thinking that they could keep slavery alive. Though most of the Civil War that erupted after that secession was fought on land, there were several important naval battles that laid the groundwork for another hundred years of honorable service for the U.S. Navy.

# A NEW BREED OF SHIP

For centuries, ships had been made of wood. Though they came in different styles, each with its own advantages and disadvantages, the material they were made of remained the same. The sight of ships wrapped in iron—and floating—shocked the people who lived near the shores of the Chesapeake Bay in Hampton Roads, Virginia. It was a March morning in 1862, and two of these iron ships were circling each other like rabid dogs in the water. Bystanders close to shore were watching in awe. Before long, the two ships began firing at each other, and the battle between the CSS *Virginia* and the USS *Monitor* had begun.

Though the U.S. Civil War was a time of strife and sorrow, it also saw advancements in naval technology, including the rise of new armored ships.

The Confederate secretary of the navy, Stephen R. Mallory, was the man behind the first ironclad constructed by the Confederacy. Mallory had seen the British and French prototypes of similar warships. He convinced the Confederate navy to recover a partially burned hull of a steam frigate called the *Merrimack*, which was then reconfigured to become an ironclad, covering it with plates of iron to protect it from cannonball fire. It was renamed the CSS *Virginia*.

Union spies quickly reported that the Confederacy was busy building a ship of the future that could defend against enemy attacks. In response, the Union started to build its own. The Union ship was designed by John Ericsson, a unique engineer who had an innovative idea for a ship made entirely of iron and shaped more like an underwater animal than a wooden ship with sails. Many Union officials doubted that his creation could even float. However, Ericsson had studied early experiments with ironclad ships; his design was based on science. He had it built in less than four months, incorporating French and British designs with his own ideas. The result was something brand-new and intimidating. His USS *Monitor* sailed into the Chesapeake Bay harbor as a fierce opponent to the Confederate's *Virginia*.

On that day in 1862, the two ships engaged each other in the morning and a dance began. The *Virginia*'s captain, Franklin Buchanan, and the *Monitor*'s captain, John Worden, dueled for more than three hours with neither side able to do much damage.

The U.S. Navy would not be as powerful as it is today without the contributions of smart thinkers like John Ericsson.

As expected, the ironclads were resistant to attack, and both ships gave up the fight by midday. The first ironclad battle was a draw.

While this first standoff produced no casualties, this new breed of ship proved its superiority to the wooden ships that were still the norm. The technologies developed and tested during the U.S. Civil War forever changed the face of naval warfare. It signaled the beginning of the end of traditional navies, and the rest of the world took notice of the ships being produced by the young United States.

# FORMAL TRAINING

When the United States was a young nation in the 1800s, Congress frequently had discussions about establishing a school that could prepare young aspiring naval officers for active duty. However, many believed that formal academic training had little value and that on-the-job training at sea was the only way to shape a capable naval officer.

The 17th secretary of the navy, George Bancroft, changed that idea. Bancroft believed that if the United States wanted to have a first-class navy, it needed a first-class school to train its officers. He was successful in obtaining a piece of land on the Severn River in Annapolis, Maryland, from the army. In 1845, the United States Naval Academy was founded and welcomed a handful of hopeful students. Nearly two centuries later, the U.S. Naval Academy is a premier college with thousands of students. Hundreds of expertly trained navy and marine corps officers graduate each year and join the fleet.

Founded in 1845, the U.S. Naval Academy has grown to become one of the most prestigious military learning centers in the world.

## TAKING CENTER STAGE

After the Civil War, the United States focused on internal issues. Similar to most postwar periods in American history, the country reduced defense spending and its military strength steeply declined. In the late 1800s, the United States began to rebuild its navy to keep up with the country's rapid industrialization and global trade routes. The United States wanted to increase the free trade of goods into and out of the country while protecting American interests overseas. At the time, Theodore Roosevelt—the assistant secretary of the navy—was heavily influ-

## MOVING BELOW THE WAVES

In the 1800s, the idea of traveling underwater had fascinated scientists and engineers for centuries. European inventors had long been investigating designs for a ship that could navigate underwater, and American inventors were equally interested. Many even tried to sell their designs to the U.S. Navy. However, the government did not become interested in "submarine" research until it was proposed that these vessels could be used to fire underwater missiles, called torpedoes, at enemy ships. An early submarine designed by H. L. Hunley was even briefly used during the Civil War; it had mixed results.

John P. Holland built his own submarine between 1895 and 1897: the USS *Plunger*, which was 85 feet (26 m) long and could carry two torpedoes. Holland's improved submarine could reach surface speeds of 15 knots and maintain a submerged speed of 8 knots.

enced by Captain Alfred Thayer Mahan, who advo-cated for sea power and sea control as the pathway by which the United States could establish itself as a world power.

The U.S. Navy also needed to be concerned with defense. When the battleship USS *Maine* was sunk by a surprise explosion off the coast of Cuba in 1898, Americans were outraged. The cry echoing through-out the halls of Congress was "Remember the *Maine*! To hell with Spain!" Before the incident, the United States was conducting negotiations to purchase Cuba and the Philippines from Spain. Cubans were revolting against Spanish control, and the *Maine* was sent to Havana Harbor to protect Americans living there. On the evening of February 15, 1898, an explosion rocked the *Maine* out of the water and destroyed its forward section. There were only 88 survivors out of a crew of more than 350 sailors. Two months later, the United States declared war on Spain. Though it was determined that the explosion was likely not caused by Spanish interference, the *Maine*'s destruction was propped up by competing newspapers to lead the country into war. Because of public outcry after the media reports, the United States found itself in a conflict that would eventually prove its power and influence around the globe. The first navy battle of the war was in Manila Bay, near the Spanish-owned Philippines.

Assistant secretary of the navy Theodore Roos-evelt appointed Commodore George Dewey as com-mander of the Asiatic Squadron. Dewey, a respected and decorated veteran of the Civil War, had a reputation for aggressive tactics and was known for taking risks. Roosevelt had high hopes that Dewey would dominate the Spanish in Manila Bay.

Commodore Dewey was confident that his heavy cruisers could outmaneuver the Spanish fleet, which was not as strong as it had been in the past. However, he was worried about some of Spain's advantages: mines in Manila Bay, the shore support the Spanish fleet would have nearby, and the distance he would

Commodore George Dewey was an imposing navy figure who helped push the United States to victory against Spain in Manila Bay.

have to travel for repairs (the closest friendly base was hundreds of miles away in Hong Kong).

Early in the morning of April 30, 1898, Dewey quietly entered Manila Bay with his small fleet of warships. They faced little resistance. The Spanish fleet had laid a trap, however, and once the American fleet was inside the bay, the enemy began firing long before Dewey's ships were even in range. The surprise attack failed, and though the Spanish fought hard, they were no match for the strengthened U.S. Navy. By the early afternoon, most of the Spanish fleet was destroyed. In a single day, Commodore Dewey had removed Spain's influence from the Pacific.

Other American naval successes during the war included the capture of Guam, a small Spanish-occupied island in the South Pacific, and the blockade of a Spanish fleet in Santiago Bay for over a month. Frustrated, the trapped Spanish fleet tried to escape the bay, guns blazing. The American ships destroyed every ship in the Spanish fleet; a little more than a month later, Spain surrendered to the United States. A century after achieving independence, American naval superiority around the world had been firmly established.

The U.S. Navy was further strengthened with the presidency of Theodore Roosevelt. As an author of a naval history of the War of 1812 and a former assistant secretary of the navy, President Roosevelt had long been a strong supporter of the navy as both a fighting force and a strong deterrent against potential enemies.

President Theodore Roosevelt supported the growth of the U.S. Navy after he was elected because he knew it would help the nation.

One of Roosevelt's earliest presidential actions was to double the budget for the navy. He also authorized the construction of many new, technologically advanced vessels to bolster the fleet. Among these new ships were battleships: huge ships with dozens of guns that were capable of firing at close, intermediate, and long ranges. As a show of growing American power, Roosevelt ordered 16 battleships be painted white and sailed all around the globe as a show of strength. Called the Great White Fleet, these ships were meant to send a message: the United States wants peace, but it is armed and ready for war.

# CHAPTER 3

# SAILING THE WORLD'S SEAS

Though the turn of the 20th century brought new advances to technology, the 1900s also plunged the world into two global conflicts of unimaginable scale. During World War I and World War II, the most powerful countries on the planet were pit against each other. Once again, the U.S. Navy was used to great effect, supporting the war effort for the United States and its allies.

In addition to these international conflicts, the United States also faced rising tension with the Soviet Union. The battlegrounds for the Cold War between these countries were found in Korea and Vietnam, where both sides sent troops to support one side of a local conflict. In the Korean War and Vietnam War, the U.S. Navy proved its flexibility by expanding its fleet to include riverine vessels to patrol the inland waterways of these nations.

# FIGHTING IN THE GREAT WAR

The early 1900s saw the first truly worldwide conflict: World War I. The battle that began in Europe did not take long to spread its destruction beyond that continent. The United States, however, attempted to stay out of the war. Americans were hesitant to get drawn into a bloody struggle that had been raging for more than three years. Opinions began to change as American merchant ships traveling across the Atlantic were being threatened by the increasing presence of German U-boats—submarines that lurked beneath the surface and could strike without warning. When a U-boat sank the civilian *Lusitania* in 1915, more than 1,000 passengers died, including 128 Americans. Though people were becoming more concerned with international affairs, the country as a whole was not eager for another war.

The United States was not eager to join World War I, but American opinions began to shift after a German U-boat attacked the *Lusitania*.

Instead of openly joining the battle, navy officers tried new tactics to protect Americans. Rear Admiral William S. Sims was one such innovator. Sims had a lot of experience interacting with Britain's Royal Navy, and he was known for being eager to try new things. In 1917, he was sold on the Royal Navy's idea of convoys. Based on a theory of "safety in numbers," the strategy involved using warships to physically escort a large group of merchant ships in a convoy. Though Sims was a believer, the tactic was controversial. Some military minds at the time thought it made the merchant ships and warships even more vulnerable—after all, a large group of ships traveling together would be even easier to find and attack. Additionally, some merchant captains feared that the risk for ship-to-ship collision would be too high if many ships had to travel so closely together. Despite some objections, the United States decided to try it.

There is little doubt that the convoy tactic worked. When ships began to travel in convoys during the summer of 1917, merchant ship sinkings and losses dropped dramatically. Convoys also gave the U.S. Navy a chance to flex its muscles. The full show of strength from American ships was meant to discourage the enemy. Eventually, however, the United States was pulled into World War I, officially entering the fray in late 1917.

Americans did not have to fight for long. World War I officially ended on November 11, 1918, a day that was named Armistice Day (now celebrated annually in the United States as Veterans Day).

During this "Great War," which lasted four years, Germany and its allies—the Central Powers—were defeated. Though the Allied Powers were the "winners," the war left Great Britain and France greatly weakened and it helped spread revolution in Russia. The social and political order of the entire continent was disrupted. In Italy and Germany, World War I set the stage for the rise of the brutal governments that would eventually spark World War II.

# GETTING MORE MOBILE

In war, mobility can be a key to victory. What if it were possible to combine the speed of an aircraft with the flexibility of a ship? Innovative naval engineers had been thinking about this question for a long time, eventually coming up with the idea of launching a plane off the deck of a ship. It made tactical sense: an aviator could be transported, via water, closer to the target location; on arrival, the aircraft could be launched with maximal fuel to accomplish the mission. Eugene Ely completed the first successful takeoff from a ship in 1910, but he had to land on a beach nearby. It was not until 1920 that a ship was actually designed for both takeoff and landing. Named after the man who conceived the idea—Samuel P. Langley—the USS *Langley* was an old collier that had been taken apart and refitted with a deck that was 542 feet (165 m) long.

Samuel P. Langley was one of the first people to successfully design and develop an aircraft carrier.

33

# ANOTHER GLOBAL BATTLE

With the rise of advanced technology in the early 1900s, it was inevitable that some countries would turn to war. However, many believed that the horrors of World War I would have been enough to prevent another global conflict. Just a few decades later, Adolf Hitler's rise to absolute power in 1930s Germany killed that belief. Hitler joined forces Italy and Japan—countries with similarly all-powerful rulers. These Axis Powers gained momentum across Europe in the late 1930s and eventually threatened democracy and freedom all around the world. The United States was again slow to join in, but after an attack on U.S. soil that destroyed a large part of the navy, the nation had little choice but to present its full force to fight the Axis Powers.

On December 7, 1941—a calm Sunday morning in Pearl Harbor, Hawaii—the day started out peacefully. The tropical harbor near the capital city of Honolulu was not considered a war zone. Rather, it was a reasonable place to stage the U.S. Pacific Fleet, since it was midway between the U.S. West Coast and Asia. Nonetheless, on December 7, Pearl Harbor became a war zone. More than 200 Japanese attack airplanes, launched from aircraft carriers in the Pacific, struck out at the navy ships at rest in the harbor. These ships were extremely vulnerable, as the United States did not consider itself at war.

The damage done was devastating. Five battleships were sunk and three more were severely

Japanese fighters flying planes like this conducted a surprise attack on Pearl Harbor in 1941, launching the United States into World War II.

disabled. It took an enormous group effort to save as many wounded sailors and sinking ships as possible.

## ENTER THE UNITED STATES

The Japanese were in a hurry. Before the Pearl Harbor attack, naval superiority in the Pacific belonged to the Japanese. However, the United States was quickly mobilizing for war; it was only a matter of time before the Americans established control. At the time, the Japanese wanted both more territory and the destruction of American aircraft carriers. By a fortunate chance, the navy carriers happened to be out to sea during the attack on Pearl Harbor. To knock out U.S. carriers, the Japanese set their sights on a small island called Midway and planned an aggressive attack. Their goal was to lure the aircraft carriers into a trap.

In advance of the assault, American codebreakers were able to decipher the date and location of the attack, helping them eliminate the element of surprise and giving them time for the U.S. Navy to prepare its own ambush. While the Japanese carpet-bombed Midway early on the morning of June 4, 1942, with little resistance, American ships approached the Japanese carriers to launch a surprise counterattack.

Despite following a good strategy, the first wave of U.S. fighters who engaged the Japanese carriers was devastated. Few of the U.S. planes made it out, but none of the Japanese planes were damaged. Luckily, this early setback still had a positive result. To attack American bombers, the Japanese fighters had dropped down to a dangerously low height. When American reinforcements arrived on the scene, they found the Japanese carriers covered with flammable debris left on the decks—and the ships were exposed, with no jet protection. American dive bombers moved in for the attack and quickly sank three of the four Japanese carriers. The Japanese struggled and fought back, but the U.S. fighters won the last round, finishing off the fourth Japanese carrier, the *Hiryu*, late that afternoon. With this battle, the entire Japanese carrier force had been destroyed in one day. A lengthy string of Japanese victories in the Pacific had come to a close. Thanks to the U.S. Navy, the tide had turned for the Allies in the Pacific theater of World War II.

# A DIFFERENT KIND OF WAR

After the United States and the Allied Powers defeated Hitler and the Axis Powers, ending World War II, the Soviet Union became determined to spread a new kind of government and economy around the world: communism. Though the United States and the Soviet Union never directly fought against each other, wars in the countries of Korea and Vietnam were seen as conflicts between the major world powers. In the 1950s and 1960s, Communists—and their handpicked North Korean and North Vietnamese leaders—dug in and began to gain power and influence over the governments in each country. In both nations, after gathering power, the Communists attempted to invade the southern half of the country. These organized efforts spread fear that the Soviets and their Communist allies wanted to dominate the world, one country at a time.

North Korean leader Kim Il-Sung was supported by Korean Communists and Soviet agents when he sent his armies across the border and invaded South Korea on June 25, 1950. Startled by the assault, the

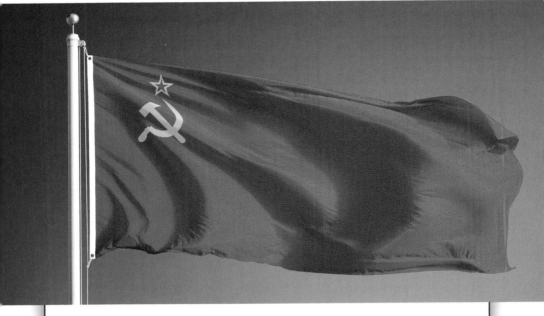

This flag, with its recognizable hammer and sickle, was a symbol of tension, fear, and anger in the United States for the latter half of the 20th century.

United Nations voted to repel the attack. The United States immediately sent ground, naval, and air units to support the South Koreans. Before long, naval and air forces began attacking the North Koreans with bombs dropped from planes and with guns mounted on navy cruisers and destroyers. The North Korean aggressors also found fierce resistance on the ground, facing South Korean fighters backed by American infantry.

These rapid military responses stabilized the situation in South Korea and prevented the North Koreans from invading further. However, they did not retreat. In response, the U.S. government determined that an amphibious landing with ground forces was necessary—and it would be behind enemy lines.

Facing the challenges of the Korean War, Rear Admiral James P. Doyle was in a tough situation. He was tasked with organizing the largest amphibious assault since the end of World War II, but the United States had decommissioned hundreds of its warships at that time in order to focus on rebuilding the American economy during peacetime. By 1950, the United States had a much smaller navy. The ships still operational were old models, without postwar technological upgrades.

Even with these considerations, Doyle successfully assembled a multinational fleet of several hundred ships. This force descended on the western coast of Korea for a showdown with North Korea and its Communist backers. The target landing site was a port town called Inchon, but the geography of the area made it almost inaccessible for an amphibious landing. The area featured wildly varying tides and was filled with outlying reefs, small islands, and shoals. The currents shifted quickly as the tides changed. Even after landing, U.S. Marines would encounter mudflats and seawalls, which they would have to traverse to fight the enemy in an industrial city the size of Omaha, Nebraska.

Challenges or not, the operation was going to proceed. After three days of "softening" up the shore with air strikes, Doyle's convoy of ships inched up the narrow channel toward the coast at Inchon on the morning of September 15, 1950. The fleet had not been able to practice for this moment, but captains were able to navigate the obstacle course and launch an advance regiment of marines. Their first action was to hoist an American flag at the top of a hill. By dawn the next morning, the American forces had taken the city of Inchon and were moving toward Seoul, the capital. The American flag was raised over Seoul two weeks later on September 27. The landing

The coastal village of Inchon was the site of one of the most important U.S. Navy operations during the Korean War.

at Inchon was a powerful victory, demonstrating how flexible the navy could be in responding quickly and aggressively to threats anywhere in the world.

It would take almost three more years of fighting before an armistice was signed on July 27, 1953, officially ending the conflict. The agreement created the Korean Demilitarized Zone (DMZ) to separate North and South Korea. Tensions between the two countries remain high to this day, and the United States maintains a presence at the DMZ to help protect South Korea.

# "UNDERWAY ON NUCLEAR POWER"

Though the word "nuclear" is most commonly associated with bombs, the rise of nuclear power in the 1950s was a major national milestone. In 1955, the USS *Nautilus* went to sea under nuclear power; it was the world's first nuclear submarine voyage. In a time period full of incredible technological accomplishments, the development of nuclear power to propel submarines is one of the most significant. The maiden voyage of the USS *Nautilus* marked the first time that submarines were truly "submersible"—nuclear power would allow these vessels to remain underwater without refueling for very long periods of time.

One driving force behind this technological breakthrough was Admiral Hyman G. Rickover, a naval officer and leading expert on nuclear propulsion. He also had a difficult personality and was not well liked. Despite his bad reputation, no one could deny Rickover's genius. His advocacy for nuclear power gave the U.S. Navy a strategic advantage.

# FROM KOREA TO VIETNAM

The Korean War ended in 1953 with neither side very happy with the outcome. In response, the Communists turned their attention to Vietnam. In 1954, Vietnamese Communists were successful in repelling the French from their country, marking an end to more than a century of colonization. Leaders then consolidated Communist power in northern Vietnam, splitting the country in two, much like Korea. To prevent the southward spread of communism, the United States began to send supplies and military advisers to South Vietnam.

The North Vietnamese had a small navy, so U.S. aircraft carriers, destroyers, and cruisers were deployed to cruise the huge coastline of Vietnam. U.S. ships also patrolled the system of rivers, canals, and estuaries in the Mekong Delta area of South Vietnam. Using smaller vessels that could rapidly move in these waterways, navy sailors inspected small boats to ensure that they were legitimate commercial traffic and not hiding enemy forces. The navy also operated a variety of other small craft in the rivers, working closely with the U.S. Army and South Vietnamese forces.

Fleets of river boats (called "patrol boats, riverine," or PBRs) did much of the heavy lifting for the navy in these dangerous, shallow waters. Their main mission was to root out and destroy guerrilla positions hidden in the jungle, but they also served as escorts for larger amphibious ships, protecting them

Vietnam is a country with thousands of miles of rivers, which were patrolled by the U.S. Navy during the Vietnam War.

from guerrilla fighters and floating mines. PBRs were dark green and just 31 feet (9 m) long. Instead of propellers, they used a water jet system, which enabled them to navigate in shallow waters. Each PBR was manned by a crew of four or five sailors and was armed with machine guns and grenade launchers. Army and navy helicopters provided air support.

One of the largest PBR firefights took place on October 31, 1966. While leading two PBR crews, Boatswain's Mate First Class James Williams stumbled upon enemy forces hiding in several boats floating ahead of him. The men on deck were wearing North Vietnamese military uniforms, so it was obvious to the PBR crews that these unidentified vessels were not being used for legitimate trade. Williams and his two boats chased and destroyed the two enemy boats. As they pursued the enemy down a narrow canal, the PBRs suddenly came upon a fleet of 40 or 50 more boats, all heavily armed and fully crewed. With little time to react, Williams decided to bombard them in a frontal assault.

Though the PBRs were small, they were strong and solidly built. The same could not be said for many North Korean vessels. Williams and his two PBRs actually ran right over several small enemy boats, crushing the flimsy structures and leaving the surprised enemies bobbing in the water. In the face of overwhelming odds, Williams and his crews emerged almost completely unscathed. He requested emergency helicopter support, then his PBRs turned around and again charged the enemy fleet. His crews, reinforced by U.S. helicopters, destroyed more than 50 enemy vessels and captured a half dozen more. Williams was awarded the Medal of Honor for his heroic efforts that day.

# THE COLD WAR UNDERWATER

The navy played a major role in the Cold War—not just in Korea and Vietnam, but also in the silent wars waged underwater between American and Soviet submarines. These engagements were a game of cat and mouse, with each country's vessels creeping around the other quietly, deep in the ocean—sometimes right under the other's nose.

This was an important job at the forefront of the Cold War. The navy men who volunteered for submarine duty spent many months away from home, living beneath the surface of the ocean. Their sacrifice played a critical role in enhancing the United States' intelligence regarding the Soviet Union's military capability. In turn, the United States was able to anticipate and deter any attack from the enemy.

## A DESERT STORM IS BREWING

After the end of the Cold War in the late 1980s, the U.S. military turned its focus to the Middle East. Tensions mounted in August 1990 when Iraqi dictator Saddam Hussein sent his army to invade the neighboring country of Kuwait. The entire world was outraged. Led by the United States, many nations became determined to help the Kuwaitis. Countries from all over the world formed a coalition force that deployed nearly half a million soldiers to repel Saddam Hussein. The U.S. Navy transported many of these troops and their equipment, bombed military targets in Iraq, and patrolled the Persian Gulf. Even in the modern age, naval superiority was important. Without strong sea support, it would be difficult to cut off Saddam Hussein's supply lines and to protect American supply lines and its oil trade.

After several weeks of an aggressive air offensive, the international coalition launched a coordinated attack against the Iraqi forces stationed in both Kuwait and Iraq. In the first 24 hours of the war, the United States flew 1,400 sorties, and American ships and submarines fired more than 100 missiles. This offensive was called Operation Desert Storm; it was supposed to form quickly, strike hard, and put an end to the war.

Just as the United States began the 20th century with a display of naval dominance led by President Roosevelt, it ended with a show of force. The power displayed by a combination of the U.S. Navy and Air Force in Operation Desert Storm was overwhelming. From hundreds of miles away, cutting-edge planes were launched from cutting-edge carriers to destroy Iraqi soldiers, Iraqi air defenses, and Iraqi infrastructure. Navy helicopters and other aircraft also routinely patrolled the Persian Gulf, keeping shipping lanes safe for civilians. The U.S. Navy, already widely respected, showed once again why it was a fighting force to be reckoned with.

# POWERFUL NEW WEAPONRY AND VICTORY

In 1991, *Los Angeles*-class fast attack submarine the USS *Louisville* (SSN-724) made naval history when it fired the first submarine-launched Tomahawk cruise missile in war. The Tomahawk cruise missile is a powerful weapon. Each missile is driven by a jet engine and is designed to effectively destroy a variety of surface targets. Tomahawks can support a wide variety of warhead, guidance, and range capabilities. With a crew of more than 100, the *Louisville* made a high-speed voyage across the Pacific and Indian Oceans to the Red Sea—traveling thousands of miles underwater—to arrive in time for battle and for the successful first launch.

Tomahawk missiles, first launched from a submarine by the USS *Louisville*, helped the United States during Operation Desert Storm.

# CHAPTER 4

# THE MODERN NAVY

The world was stunned when the United States suffered a deadly terrorist attack on September 11, 2001. Planes had been hijacked by extremists and flown into the World Trade Center (in New York City) and the Pentagon (outside of Washington, D.C.), killing nearly 3,000 people and kicking off a multinational conflict that would stretch for more than a decade. After these attacks, the United States declared a "war on terrorism," deploying thousands of Americans from all service branches to countries in the Middle East.

As always, the navy has done its part in defense of the nation. Navy airstrikes have destroyed enemy infrastructure, navy vessels have patrolled the region's waterways, navy SEALs have battled insurgents, and navy doctors, nurses, and hospital corpsmen have tended to the wounded. In addition, the navy has deployed engineers and builders to construct bases and other structures in support of the war effort.

# NAVY SEALS WITH A TOUGH JOB

As the most elite fighters in the U.S. Navy, the SEALs are often tasked with dangerous, difficult missions far behind enemy lines. For many years, the United States and its allies had been searching for Osama bin Laden, a Saudi Arabian man who was responsible for planning and organizing the September 11 attacks. When credible intelligence about his location finally came through in 2011—nearly a decade after the attacks—navy SEALs were called upon to hunt him down.

The risky mission to capture or kill bin Laden was called Operation Neptune Spear. Flying modified Black Hawk helicopters, two teams of SEALs silently passed the border between Afghanistan and Pakistan in May 2011. The target was a walled compound that held bin Laden, one of the greatest enemies the United States had ever seen. Though they had little intelligence about who would be inside the house, the SEALs carried out their mission with courage, leading to the eventual death of bin Laden. The entire raid took less than 40 minutes.

## AIRCRAFT CARRIER POWER

Naval technology has come a long way since the days of plain wooden ships. Perhaps nothing symbolizes the power and strength of the U.S. Navy more than the modern aircraft carrier. The United States has invested billions of dollars to research, develop, test, construct, and maintain its huge fleet of aircraft carriers. For an enemy, these vessels are a frightening sight on the horizon. In addition to being useful—and

Enormous, powerful, and expensive, the modern aircraft carrier is a true sign of naval strength.

powerful—in a fight, they help deter conflict just as President Roosevelt's Great White Fleet did in the early 1900s.

U.S. presidents always ask their military leaders where the nation's carriers are when faced with an international crisis. The commander in chief relies on the aircraft carriers as the centerpiece of the U.S. Navy to protect the nation's interests at home and abroad. The nation's leaders count on these gigantic, floating runways to support and operate aircraft that engage in attack, surveillance, and electronic warfare against targets at sea, in the air, or ashore. Each of these massive ships leads a "battle group" of navy power that includes cruisers, destroyers, submarines, and frigates, plus several squadrons of aircraft. Battle groups often rest off the shores of potentially hostile foreign countries, sending a clear message to enemies of the United States.

The USS *George Washington* is a shining example of the modern aircraft carrier. It measures in at 1,092 feet (333 m) long, 257 feet (78 m) wide, and 244 feet (74 m) high, with a weight of 97,000 tons (88,000 metric tons). Its crew comprises more than 5,000 sailors and aviators, and it carries nearly 100 aircraft aboard. The ship has enough food to serve close to 20,000 meals a day while at sea, and it contains a distilling plant that can process 400,000 gallons (1,500,000 L) of fresh water each day. It is truly a small city, complete with doctors, dentists, pilots, lawyers, plumbers, mechanics, chemists, weather forecasters, air traffic controllers, security guards, journalists, photographers, barbers, cooks, and a host of other specialists—all living together on board. When these men and women are called for deployment, they leave their families for six or more months at a time.

While aircraft carriers and the ships, submarines, and aircraft that accompany them focus on protecting the seas and sending air power ashore, the navy performs many other missions to protect the nation, defend U.S. interests, and help those in need.

# LIFE ON A CARRIER

What is it like to work on an aircraft carrier today? In short, the days are long and the pace is fast. The center of activity is the flight deck: a small airport and landing strip that can "launch" a plane every 45 seconds. When the ship is at sea, the sailors assigned to the flight deck scurry around almost 24 hours a day. Each flight deck crew member is a part of a coordinated "ballet," a detailed series of directions to move the maximum number of planes on and off the deck in the shortest amount of time possible.

Catapult officers, for example, help launch and land different types of aircraft. Carrier catapults, as their name implies, are slingshots that can propel a 36-ton (33 mt) aircraft off the bow of the ship into the air. When planes finish their missions and fly back to the ship, they lower their tail hook, a big loop of metal attached to the underside of the aircraft. This hook connects to arresting wire, which is a long line that is stretched taut across the width of the ship. This wire stops the aircraft in 200 feet (61 m)—much shorter than a runway seen at a traditional airport.

## MUCH MORE THAN FIGHTING

With the ability to rapidly mobilize and send people anywhere in the world, the U.S. Navy has often played a role in world relief efforts. The navy provided support after the 2004 tsunami in Indonesia, Hurricane Katrina on the Gulf Coast in 2005, the 2010 earthquake in Haiti, the 2015 earthquake in Nepal, and many other natural disasters.

Crew members from the aircraft carrier USS *Abraham Lincoln* worked around the clock in the Aceh Province in Sumatra, Indonesia, to ensure that vital food, water, and medical supplies were carried to survivors of the 2004 tsunami. They used the ship's trucks, helicopters, and hands to get the supplies from the coast deep into isolated villages and towns.

When Hurricane Katrina devastated New Orleans, the USS *Iwo Jima* pulled into port soon after the storm. The vessel became a center for relief efforts, offering assistance to those trapped, lost, or injured.

When a powerful earthquake hit the island nation of Haiti on January 12, 2010, the nation was devastated. The navy responded immediately with more than 10,000 sailors and marines, 17 ships, 48 helicopters, and 12 aircraft. Soldiers delivered relief supplies for distribution to affected areas. In addition, the hospital ship USNS *Comfort* was sent with supplies, facilities, and skilled medical personnel equivalent to a complete hospital.

Though its primary function is to fight to defend the United States, the navy is also often used to help those in need after natural disasters.

Similarly, when Nepal was struck by an earthquake in 2015, the navy was quick to deploy troops to help out. In addition to offering food and medical supplies, the navy also helped train Nepalese soldiers so they may better prepare for future natural disasters.

## THE NAVY'S STRUCTURE

The United States military was specifically designed so that civilians always oversee it. This policy ensures that a powerful military leader cannot take control of the country. The organizational relationship between the president of the United States and the navy is shaped like a pyramid, with the president at the top. U.S. presidents take the title commander in chief as part of the job, which means that they are the commander of all military actions taken by the country.

Directly reporting to the president is the secretary of defense, who is a civilian appointed by the president. The secretary of defense acts as an executive officer of all the service branches: the U.S. Army, Air Force, Coast Guard, Marine Corps, Navy, and Space Force. Reporting to the secretary of defense is the secretary of the navy, also a civilian appointed by the president. The secretary of the navy oversees the navy and the marine corps. At the next level down is the navy's highest-ranked military officer (a four-star admiral), who is called the chief of naval operations, or CNO.

As the highest-ranking sailor in the country, the chief of naval operations is responsible for overseeing the navy's missions.

Among the highest-ranking officials in the entire United States are the joint chiefs of staff (JCS). The JCS group was created from the National Security Act of 1947 because the government believed there should be a more formal joint command structure. As a member of the JCS, the CNO is the primary adviser to the president and the secretary of defense on the conduct of naval warfare. The CNO is also the principal administrative adviser to the secretary of the navy.

The United States military is divided into several geographically based commands: U.S. Northern

Command, U.S. Pacific Command, U.S. Southern Command, U.S Central Command, and the U.S. European Command. Every one of these commands controls fleets of ships, aircraft, submarines, bases, and sailors. When the navy moves around the world at sea, it usually travels in groups of ships, aircraft, and submarines.

## NAVY GROUPINGS

Wherever the navy finds itself, aircraft carriers are at the center of attention. A carrier often accompanies a group of ships traveling together in support of American foreign policy abroad. In addition to an aircraft carrier, a battle group typically includes cruisers (surface ships used primarily for anti-air warfare) and destroyers and frigates (surface ships used mainly for antisubmarine warfare). Standard groups also include a fast attack submarine, which is deployed primarily to seek out and destroy hostile surface ships; other submarines; and a supply ship that carries ammunition, oil, and other equipment.

In addition, the aircraft carrier hosts a carrier air wing. As part of these massive vessels, the air wing includes fighter aircraft, attack aircraft, antisubmarine fighting aircraft (both jets and helicopters), surveillance aircraft, and cargo aircraft.

In addition to carrier battle groups, the U.S. Navy also uses expeditionary strike groups to support its mission overseas. A group of this nature will consist of strike-capable surface warships and submarines, which are increasingly being used in areas of smaller threats. These warships typically include amphibious ships (to carry and deliver marines and helicopters to shore), cruisers, destroyers, frigates, and submarines.

Every navy vessel, regardless of class, is crewed by both officers and enlisted sailors, all of whom work closely together to make the ship run smoothly. There are more than 320,000 people actively serving in the navy. The vast majority are enlisted sailors who joined the navy right out of high school, or those who are older but do not have a college degree. Around 50,000 men and women serve as officers, placed in charge of groups of enlisted sailors. Officers are required to have a college degree, and they are responsible for leading and teaching those who serve beneath them. Even a junior-grade lieutenant officer, with only one to four years of experience in the navy, could be responsible for overseeing several dozen enlisted men and women.

In addition to members of the navy who serve at the front lines of conflict, there are thousands of people who work in support roles to keep equipment in good shape. When vessels are docked in ports at navy bases across the globe, members of the base staff help out with maintenance tasks. There are also people who work in office buildings at bases, handling the administrative portions of the workload by filling out paperwork and performing other important—if rarely discussed—tasks.

# CHAPTER 5

# STRONGER FOR DIVERSITY

Today's armed services are a welcoming community for people of all genders, races, and orientations. Everyone who wants to serve in the U.S. Navy—and has the ability to do so—is accepted with open arms. However, things were not always so equal. For most of the navy's history, women primarily served as support staff or nurses. Beginning in the 1900s, however, female sailors began to make their mark working on ships and flying planes in the navy.

People of color have been directly involved in U.S. naval operations for more than two centuries, though they often had to serve in noncombat roles or in units segregated from white soldiers. After World War II, the navy began to integrate people of all races into one unified fighting force, and that decision has paid off. The modern navy is a powerful global force because it allows people of all backgrounds to work side by side.

# FROM THE SEA TO THE STARS

Captain Wendy Lawrence has always been a trailblazer. After she graduated from the U.S. Naval Academy in one of the first classes to allow females, she became a naval aviator. In her career, Lawrence logged more than 1,500 hours of flight time in six different helicopters and conducted more than 800 ship landings. In 1992, NASA selected her to undergo astronaut training. She spent more than 1,200 hours in space, including as part of the 2005 STS-114 *Discovery* flight.

Captain Wendy Lawrence is just one of the many women with navy backgrounds to achieve great things.

# NOT JUST FOR MEN

For much of the history of the United States, women primarily worked with the armed forces as nurses and surgical assistants. They cared for soldiers wounded in combat and helped run military hospitals. In 1908, Congress authorized the establishment of a Navy Nurse Corps, formally carving out a role for American women nurses in the navy to serve both at home and abroad.

When the United States entered World War I, there was a severe labor force shortage, so women were recruited to fill jobs not at the fighting fronts. In addition to expanded roles in nursing, the navy accepted its first enlisted women soldiers as "yeomanettes" (an unofficial version of the normal "yeoman" rank). Women were also allowed to serve as Marine Reservists, providing administrative and clerical support. Many considered enlisted life an unusual step for women to take at the time, but their patriotism and desire to help their country helped turn the tide of the war.

After the United States entered World War II, all the military branches were looking for people to cover the jobs left by men who were sent overseas to fight the Axis Powers. The obvious choice was for women to begin serving in expanded roles. The United States created a program called Women Accepted for Voluntary Emergency Service (WAVES) and some 300,000 women stepped up to support the nation's war effort.

In the peacetime that followed World War II, the number of women in the navy—and the types of jobs they performed—was reduced. Despite their excellent service in World War I and World War II, in the mid-1900s, women were generally workers around the home. As conflicts in Korea and Vietnam broke out, however, the armed forces once again called for the expertise and experience of navy nurses, who were sent to war zones in increasing numbers. It was not until the early 1970s that women were permitted to venture onto ships and aircraft as regular crew members. Around the same time, feminist movements were sweeping the country, fueling demands to allow women to work jobs that were previously unavailable to them. This led to the end of the WAVES and the full integration of women into the U.S. Navy.

Since the 1970s, women have served with distinction and earned jobs at every level of the U.S. Navy. Fairly early on, women were allowed to take aviation training to fly naval aircraft, with the first graduate—Lieutenant Barbara Allen—qualifying in 1974. Women first enrolled in the U.S. Naval Academy in 1976. In 1994, women were flying combat aircraft and they were permitted to be permanently assigned to aircraft carriers. The first woman to command a navy warship was Captain Kathleen McGrath, who took command of the USS *Jarrett* in 2000. In 2010, the Department of the Navy changed its policy and opened the doors for qualified women to serve on submarines. The first group of nuclear-trained women officers started serving on ballistic missile submarines—larger than agile attack submarines—in 2011. In January 2015, the first group of women reported aboard the fast attack submarine USS *Minnesota*.

Women from all service branches played a large role in Operations Desert Shield and Desert Storm, which deployed more than 500,000 servicemen and women to the Persian Gulf. Navy women served in a variety of roles on ammunition and supply ships; on helicopters; in construction jobs; and at fleet hospitals as doctors, nurses, and corpsmen. As in past conflicts, female sailors served admirably and honorably.

Some have observed that the changing nature of warfare—especially conflicts in the Middle East that followed the September 11, 2001, attacks—is opening doors for women. For many years, female soldiers were not allowed to serve on fighting fronts. However, with the power and speed of modern weapons, women stationed at combat hospitals or supply depots are equally at risk as the men in the field. In 2015, for the first time, the United States began permitting women to serve in frontline infantry combat roles.

## THE POWER OF DIVERSITY

The modern armed forces are a welcoming community for people of all races, but prior to the late 1900s, the United States had a difficult time

Though they have been given equal access to opportunities for only a few decades, female sailors have consistently confirmed their value in the military.

accepting minorities. While Black Americans have been serving in the navy since the beginning, they were historically stationed to work in the galleys and the engine rooms. Discrimination and unfair policies prevented them from serving alongside white sailors. When Black sailors were allowed to fight, they had to work out of segregated units. After World War II, however, Congress changed the laws to allow all servicemen and women—regardless of race—to serve in regular, integrated units. Since then, minorities have increasingly served in all ranks and designations.

Black sailors have played a significant role in U.S. naval history. In 1944, a group of 13 officers were commissioned as the first Black navy officers in history. Ensign Jesse LeRoy Brown became the first Black naval aviator when he received his wings of gold in 1948. In 1949, Commander Wesley A. Brown was the first Black American to graduate from the Naval Academy. Vice Admiral Samuel Lee Gravely Jr. became the first Black commander of a navy fighting ship when he earned command of the USS *Falgout* in 1962. In 1971, Gravely also became the first Black admiral. In 1999, Admiral Michelle Howard became the first Black woman to command a navy ship, the USS *Rushmore*. Howard was also the first Black woman to achieve four-star rank in the U.S. armed forces.

Inspired by the achievements of others, many Black Americans heard the call to serve in the navy. By 1992, Black Americans made up a larger percentage of the navy's population than they did

Admiral Michelle Howard is one of the most accomplished sailors in U.S. history, male or female.

of the general U.S. population. By opening more career paths to people of color, the navy found itself refreshed with a stronger fighting force. Native Americans and Americans of Hispanic, Asian, Arabic, and other heritages have also been key contributors to the U.S. Navy. Hispanic sailors have served in every U.S. conflict since the American Revolution. Civil War admiral David Farragut, who helped defeat the Confederate forces at the Battle of Mobile Bay, was of Spanish descent. Everett Alvarez Jr., a Mexican American, was the longest-held prisoner during the Vietnam War.

Filipinos have been serving in the U.S. Navy since the 1800s, but it was not until Susan Ahn Cuddy—a Korean American—became a gunnery officer and intelligence officer in World War II that the navy could claim its first Asian American officer. Rear Admiral Joseph J. Clark, a Cherokee, was the first Native American to graduate from the Naval Academy.

Today, the U.S. Navy is respected around the globe as the world's premier maritime fighting force. Though technological advances have played a large part in the navy's rise to dominance, equally important were its leaders' decisions to allow women and people of color to serve alongside white men. Modern navy ships strongly represent the American promise: people of all races, beliefs, orientations, and backgrounds serving alongside one another to protect the nation.

# A WOMAN OF FIRSTS

Admiral Michelle Howard has military blood running through her veins. The daughter of a master sergeant in the air force, Howard graduated from the U.S. Naval Academy in 1982. She quickly learned to take on a lot of responsibility. She became the first Black woman to earn command of a navy ship, and she was also the first Black woman to achieve a three-star and four-star rank. She eventually went on to become the vice chief of naval operations—the second-highest rank in the navy—making her the highest-ranked women in the history of the branch.

# CHAPTER 6

# LEARNING TO SERVE

In the middle of the 20th century, the United States relied on a draft to populate the ranks of the army, navy, air force, marines, and coast guard. In this system, all males were required to register for military duty at the age of 18. Names were periodically selected at random, and any man whose name was called was forced to serve. Though there were still voluntary enlistees, many armed forces were staffed by people who were drafted.

The draft was widely unpopular, and the modern U.S. service branches are volunteer only. Adult males must still register for a program called the Selective Service, but since this new system has been implemented, it has never been used to force Americans to serve. Most agree that the military, including the navy, is stronger because it accepts only those who truly want to join. But what happens when someone decides they want to become a sailor?

# BECOMING ELIGIBLE

Anyone who wants to serve in the U.S. Navy must be at least 18 years old, a U.S. citizen, and a high school graduate (or hold a GED). Navy officers must hold a college degree or be working toward one. Because its sailors are meant to be a strong fighting force, the navy also imposes strict physical fitness requirements. Some are general, which everyone must meet, and some are specific to certain jobs. For instance, pilots must have excellent eyesight; navy SEALs must pass extremely difficult fitness tests and be outstanding swimmers. Some jobs in the navy also demand a certain educational background. A submarine officer, for example, must have a strong education in engineering and science.

No matter where a sailor serves, the navy requires its members to be drug free. There is no tolerance for drug use in the navy, and using drugs is grounds for immediate disqualification. Young servicemen and women should expect to face drug tests both routinely and randomly.

Semiannual physical readiness tests are administered to every sailor in the navy. Everyone must pass this test twice a year in order to remain in the navy. To pass these tests, it is important for sailors to maintain a healthy, balanced diet, exercise regularly, and refrain from smoking and excessive drinking.

# FROM RECRUITMENT TO BOOT CAMP

The first step toward joining the navy is to get in touch with a navy recruiter. Located in offices all over the United States, a recruiter's job is to help interested young men and women enlist as sailors and officers. A recruiter can answer questions about life in the navy, and if a candidate decides to join, the recruiter will guide them through the application and selection process.

Once a young person is selected for service— whether as an enlisted sailor or an officer—they must go through intense training. Enlisted personnel are required to successfully complete navy boot camp, a 10-week, full-time training course that teaches new recruits the basics of a soldier's life, including how to wear a uniform and work on a ship. It also forces recruits to achieve a high level of physical fitness.

For young aspiring officers, the pathway is a little different. To enter the navy at a higher rank, recruits are required to earn an officer's commission. There are three ways to receive a commission: the U.S. Naval Academy, Naval Reserve Officers' Training Corps (NROTC), and Officer Candidate School (OCS). The Naval Academy is difficult to get into and is the most demanding of the options, as it requires individuals to commit themselves to naval training full-time for four years. Just one of many benefits of the Naval Academy is that officer candidates receive an excellent college education for free while they work toward their commission. The NROTC option allows individuals to attend any university to which they are accepted and gives them part-time naval officer training while attending college. Some NROTC candidates also receive help with college tuition. OCS gives those who are already college graduates the opportunity to become officers by completing 13 weeks of full-time training.

Attending and completing a lengthy boot camp is one tradition common among all branches of the armed forces. At navy boot camp, recruits are trained both on land and at sea. They must pass a series of physical tests that include push-ups, sit-ups, and a 1.5-mile (2.4 km) run. There are also swimming tests, which include jumping into the water from at least 5 feet (1.5 m) high, remaining afloat for five minutes, and swimming at least 50 yards (45 m). As they improve their fitness, recruits will learn first aid, communications, and how to identify different ships and aircraft. About halfway through boot camp, recruits are given weapons training, including live fire exercises. On board a ship, firefighting and other damage-control skills are learned and drilled.

The final boot camp challenge for navy recruits is the "battle stations" test. This exercise has 12 different stages and tests a recruit's knowledge and the physical abilities they gained during boot camp. During the whole battle stations test, men and women wear a baseball cap labeled "Recruit." However, once they complete the challenge, they have the honor of wearing a cap with their new label: "Navy."

Boot camp is a challenging training program, but it helps recruits toughen up physically and mentally.

This change is a symbol of their transformation into sailors. Following battle stations, the recruits graduate in full uniform at an official ceremony, ready to begin their careers in the navy.

After graduation from boot camp, each sailor must complete extensive training that will prepare them for a designated specialty. This training can last several months or several years, depending on the type of specialty pursued. For example, a navy pilot will spend several years training almost full-time to learn to fly a fighter aircraft. Even after earning their wings, young navy pilots are considered novices until they have spent a few years in the fleet, earning experience at sea and in combat. However, pilot is only one of the career options open to young sailors. Each unique specialty within the navy offers sailors a path of increasing responsibilities and demonstrated skills over the course of a career that can last for decades.

## UP IN THE AIR

Since 1910, when Eugene Ely catapulted his plane from the platform of a ship for the first time, the navy has produced several generations of highly qualified aviators who are proud to wear the navy wings of gold. Naval officers who pursue an aviation specialty can become pilots and fly aircraft, or they can become naval flight officers (NFOs) and control the aircraft's weapons and guidance systems. These highly trained officers can find themselves performing a variety of missions for the navy, either on ship-based jets or on land-based transport planes. Typical missions assigned to pilots include fleet air defense, air-to-air fighting, ground attack, antisubmarine warfare, and search-and-rescue operations.

Earning the wings of gold is not easy. Those who wish to become pilots or NFOs must become naval officers before they can attend primary and advanced flight training programs. Because their training is longer and more specialized, these highly respected pilots and NFOs also have longer service obligations. This means they must serve for a relatively long period of time before they are allowed to retire from the navy.

Though pilots and NFOs get most of the attention, naval aviation requires a large support crew of technically trained enlisted personnel who specialize in aircraft mechanics, weapons handling, navigation, meteorology, flight safety, and engine systems. Naval aviation would not be possible without these important specialists.

Many aspire to earn the navy wings of gold, but only the best of the best can become full-time aviators.

# ON THE SURFACE, BELOW THE SEA

Many young sailors dream of issuing orders as a commander at sea. Surface warfare officers (SWOs) are dedicated professionals who train their whole careers to command a fighting surface ship. SWOs are responsible for overseeing the entire crew and ensuring the success of all operations. After earning their commissions, naval officers who want to become SWOs are immediately sent to work aboard a surface ship. While assigned to their first ship, they attend Surface Warfare Officers School and continue to set sail in roles of increasing responsibility on a variety of surface ships, including destroyers, cruisers, frigates, minesweepers, aircraft carriers, patrol boats, supply ships, and oilers. Today's navy SWOs have a proud legacy in U.S. history.

SWOs are at the top, but surface ships also rely on their crews of highly trained enlisted specialists. The support personnel comprises boatswain's mates, operations specialists, electrician's mates, enginemen, machinist's mates, fire-control technicians, intelligence specialists, quartermasters, signalmen, and yeomen, just to name a few.

Surface ships are not the only navy fish in the water. Since Admiral Hyman Rickover launched the USS *Nautilus* in 1955, the U.S. has maintained a fleet of submarines under the command of the navy. Submarines come in two design types that are on duty under the ocean 24 hours a day, 365 days a year: fast attack submarines (SSNs) and ballistic missile submarines (SSBNs).

The SSN-688 *Los Angeles*-class fast attack submarine is the backbone of the navy's attack submarine force. These vessels travel in the open ocean at high speeds, patrolling the seas and observing enemy activity all over the world. They are 360 feet (110 m) long, can travel at 20 knots, and can carry 133 people. The SSN-21 *Seawolf*-class fast attack submarine is specifically designed to perform high-speed, deep-depth submerged operations. The *Seawolf* is quieter than the *Los Angeles*-class submarines.

The *Ohio*-class Trident fleet ballistic missile submarine is a key part of America's nuclear force. These vessels are capable of carrying nuclear weapons and responding to any enemy nuclear threat. They are 560 feet (170 m) long, can travel submerged at more than 20 knots, and can carry 155 people.

Naval officers who want to one day learn how to command an SSN or SSBN must receive special training on nuclear power and submarine warfare. Most submarine officers have strong technical, science, and engineering educational backgrounds.

Submarines are incredible pieces of technology, and they require the support of a dedicated crew to work properly. Submarine support specialists include sonar technicians (responsible for listening to and detecting underwater movement of other ships and submarines), weapons handlers, cryptologists (responsible for collecting and analyzing intelligence data), oceanographic specialists, weather forecasters, and nuclear power-plant technicians.

# "LITTORAL" FIGHTING

As conflicts are increasingly being fought close to shore (instead of on the open ocean), the U.S. government has been investing more resources to build ships that can be used in shallower waters. The country's first littoral combat ship (LCS) was appropriately named USS *Freedom*. LCSs like the *Freedom* are smaller than traditional surface ships, making them faster and easier to maneuver in shallow waters that are currently inaccessible to traditional naval ships. LCSs are also highly advanced, capable of being equipped with different modules that can be reconfigured to suit a variety of missions. LCS vessels are capable of landing special operations and maritime interdiction forces, as well as intelligence and reconnaissance teams. Though smaller than normal surface ships, they can still transport helicopters, small boats, and unmanned air, surface, and subsurface vehicles.

Smaller and quicker than their seafaring counterparts, LCSs are a new variety of navy war ship.

# FRESH SUBS

Submarines are some of the modern world's most powerful weapons, and the U.S. Navy has wasted no time building up its fleet of unique vessels. Two of the newest breeds of submarine are the *Virginia* class (SSN-774) of fast attack submarines, the *Seawolf* class (SSN-21) of attack submarines, and a modified Trident ballistic missile submarine—a guided missile submarine, or SSGN. The *Virginia*-class SSN is capable of many of the same missions as the *Los Angeles*-class submarines but is uniquely designed for use in littoral and regional operations. *Seawolf* submarines are very quiet and very fast, are equipped with advanced sensors, and can carry up to 50 weapons in their torpedo rooms. The mighty new SSGNs have been reconfigured to carry more than 160 Tomahawk land-attack missiles, giving these submarines the ability to conduct large-volume strikes.

Modern submarines are technological wonders that combine strength and stealth to accomplish the navy's missions.

# TAKING CARE

Serving in the armed forces can be a dangerous job. The navy has a team of medical professionals—doctors, nurses, dentists, hospital corpsmen, and medical service corps—who provide care for the navy and the marines. These individuals are highly trained, often by the navy. In exchange for advanced medical training, they agree to serve in the navy for several years, caring for fellow sailors or marines. Their duties do not stop at providing medical attention, however. Navy doctors have dual roles as combat-trained naval sailors and as caregivers to the sick and injured. This dual responsibility makes those who serve in navy medicine unique professionals.

While most of the navy's doctors become medical specialists, they are first and foremost military physicians. That means that they must be prepared to be deployed and work in operational or emergency medicine. They tend to soldiers wounded in combat, and their rapid attention can be the difference between life and death.

Hospital corpsmen serve a unique role: though they technically work for the navy, they support the marine corps (a separate branch of the armed forces). In combat, hospital corpsmen serve in marine units as emergency medical technicians who provide triage and first aid to wounded and sick servicemen and women.

# NURSES AND DENTISTS

Founded in 1908, the Navy Nurse Corps has a long history of providing medical care at hospitals, in clinics, aboard ships, and in field hospitals around the world. These dedicated men and women work closely with navy medical officers, dental officers, and hospital corpsmen. Like civilian nurses, navy nurses can find themselves working in emergency room and trauma medicine, general surgery, neurosurgery, obstetrics/gynecology, orthopedics, pediatrics, or psychiatry.

Established by Congress in 1912, the Navy Dental Corps is a proud group of dental professionals who pioneer cutting-edge dental techniques and advanced technology. With more than a dozen Naval Dental Centers around the United States, Puerto Rico, Guam, Italy, and Japan—plus dental officers and dental hygienists on board most large ships—the navy is capable of providing onsite dental care to sailors assigned all over the world.

There are several ways to become a navy medical or dental professional. Because the services they provide are invaluable, many doctors, dentists, and nurses can receive direct financial help from the U.S. government to pay for their education. In return, after receiving a medical license, young physicians and nurses must serve in the armed forces for a set number of years. Though it is permitted to attend a civilian university for a medical, dental, or nursing degree, there is also a Uniformed Services University of the Health Sciences (USUHS). The USUHS is the military's own medical and graduate nursing school, located in Bethesda, Maryland.

Some candidates have already earned their degrees before they enter the navy. Those selected for their respective programs are sent to Officer Indoctrination School, which is a short course in how to be a naval officer. In five weeks, the navy trains these medical professionals in effective management styles, leadership techniques, navy history and policies, and how to wear a uniform.

The navy's dedicated health care professionals go through just as much training and education as their combat counterparts.

As elite fighters, navy SEALs have earned a reputation for operating fast with great efficiency—and lethality.

## THE ELITE SEALS

One of the most selective and demanding specialties in the navy—and ranking among the most dangerous navy professions—navy SEALs must be prepared to operate in any arena, whether it is at SEa, in the Air, or on Land. This is where their name originates.

Because SEALs are supposed to be ready to jump into action at a moment's notice, they must undergo training that is both mentally and physically challenging. This training produces the world's best maritime warriors. Those interested in becoming a SEAL must first complete boot camp and learn to be a sailor (or become an officer). Then, SEAL candidates undergo a six-month program called Basic Underwater Demolition/SEAL (BUD/S) Training in Coronado, California. This next step of training focuses on physical conditioning, small boat handling, diving physics, basic diving techniques, land warfare, weapons, demolitions, communications, and reconnaissance.

## WORKING IN SUPPORT

Though the U.S. Navy is primarily meant to be a fighting force, there are many jobs available to those who do not want to serve on the front lines. Naval Mobile Construction Battalions (NMCBs)—also called SeaBees—provide engineering support for the navy. SeaBees are highly trained construction specialists that can be deployed anywhere around the world to build airfields, staging areas, hospitals, bridges, and many other logistical structures in support of the navy and the marine corps.

Judge advocate generals—or JAGs—are the military's dedicated team of lawyers. A young navy JAG corps officer can be arguing cases in a courtroom within 120 days of beginning active duty. All major commands have JAGs, who are trained as both military officers and as lawyers, to advise personnel on all legal matters. They provide legal assistance for consumer protection, real estate transactions, federal and state taxes, domestic disputes, and financial counseling. Military and maritime law is different from civilian law and requires specially trained individuals.

The Navy Supply Corps comprises highly trained professionals who perform executive-level duties in financial management, inventory control, physical distribution systems, contracting, computer systems, material logistics, retailing, and food service. The Supply Corps orders the fuel, the hamburgers, the ammunition, and the toilet paper to provision aircraft carriers and other ships. Without the Supply Corps officers' expertise in inventory, logistics, and distribution systems, the U.S. Navy's ships, bases, and other facilities could not function.

Information about potential enemies is extremely valuable in the modern age of warfare. In the military, this information is known as "intelligence." The navy trains and employs intelligence officers to track, collect, and analyze knowledge about an

Keeping the navy adequately provisioned is a difficult job, but the Supply Corps works to make sure that sailors have what they need when they need it.

enemy's capabilities and plans. They are commissioned officers who receive specialized training on how to get the most out of the data they can find. Intelligence officers commonly work in embassies around the world, aboard ships, and in the Pentagon. Serving below intelligence officers are intelligence specialists, the enlisted personnel who also work in this field in support of the officers, typically helping analyze and present information.

Religious freedom is one of the cornerstones of the United States, and the navy employs clergy members called chaplains to represent many faiths. For more than two centuries, the navy's Chaplain Corps has been assigned to hospitals, ships, the marines, and the coast guard. The Chaplain Corps is responsible for providing religious support and counseling services to servicemen and women during both war and peacetime. Religious program specialists are the enlisted personnel who assist navy chaplains with administrative and budgetary tasks.

The navy also employs a variety of other specialists—most of whom receive their training in the navy. Other specialists include divers, photographers, journalists, security guards, cooks, small-boat handlers, musicians, postal clerks, sonar and radar technicians, electricians, meteorologists, firefighters, navigators, information technology (IT) specialists, construction workers, accountants, and teachers. The navy routinely trains those who enlist right after high school to fill these jobs. All perform vital roles for the navy at sea and ashore.

Every day, sailors train to react to any emergency. This fire drill on the deck of a destroyer shows the crew working together.

# NAVY RELATIONSHIPS

Though the marine corps and the navy are separate and distinct uniformed services, the marine corps technically falls under the Department of the Navy. As a seafaring force, the navy specializes in battle and transport on the open water. The marine corps is typically called on to provide the navy with landing forces for amphibious and land-based operations. The marine corps and the navy have a historically close relationship. The navy relies on the marine corps to transform sea power into land power, and the marine corps depends on the navy to transport soldiers and supplies in expeditionary missions around the world. Navy hospital corpsmen also provide medical care for marine corps units.

The navy also has a special relationship with the U.S. Coast Guard. Though the U.S. Coast Guard— the smallest of the country's main armed service branches—generally works under the authority of the Department of Homeland Security, the Department of the Navy takes over during wartime (or at the direction of the president). In regular duty, ships of the coast guard are responsible for keeping U.S. harbors, riverways, and—of course—coasts safe. They are often called on to perform search-and-rescue missions and regulate local maritime vessels. In the 21st century, the coast guard has taken on more of an international role, working alongside the navy to provide sea-based support to missions in the Middle East and around the globe.

As the nation's two maritime military branches, the U.S. Navy and the Coast Guard work closely together every day.

# CHAPTER 7

# THE FUTURE OF NAVAL WARFARE

The war on terrorism, which kicked off following the September 11 attacks, has reached well beyond its original scope of fighting a few isolated terror groups. This decades-long conflict has been difficult for American servicemen and servicewomen, including those from the U.S. Navy, who have sometimes been deployed in faraway countries for months at a time, cut off from friends and family. However, this new breed of warfare has brought along many technological advancements that will forever change the face of naval fighting. Nuclear power, mighty aircraft carriers, unmanned aerial vehicles, and cyberwarfare are just a few of the newer fields in which members of the navy can serve. There has never been a better time for a young person to become a sailor.

# FUTURE FIGHTING

Since it was founded in the late 1700s, the backbone of the navy has always been its vessels that can be deployed in the open ocean. Though times have changed and wooden ships have been replaced by aircraft carriers and nuclear submarines, the principle is the same. However, in recent years, the navy has increasingly been using riverine vessels that can patrol the coastal and inland waterways in foreign countries. Like many other armed forces, the navy is also deploying unmanned aerial vehicles—or drones—which are remote-controlled devices that can observe enemy activity on land, at sea, and under the water, all without putting a single sailor at risk. As U.S. military branches continue to improve their cooperation, it will likely not be uncommon to see navy aircraft carriers transporting air force planes and army helicopters. The navy will also continue to expand its special operations forces, training soldiers who can become world leaders in urban warfare, hostage rescue, and highly secret operations while working in small groups.

All this advancement means that the future looks bright for any young person who dreams of becoming a member of the U.S. Navy. Improved technology will lead to new specialties in engineering, maintenance, computer science, and more. On top of that, there is always a need for physically fit, mentally tough, and hard-working young sailors who can put their heads down and work in support roles aboard the

Drone warfare is one of the newest additions to the navy's arsenal of weapons and tactics.

country's ships. The navy offers training courses for a huge number of specialties, which makes it easy for a young person to find a career path that fits their interests—whether they spend an entire career in the military or rejoin civilian life after their first enlistment period ends. The U.S. Navy has ships just beyond every horizon, carrying soldiers and supplies all over the world. There is a place on any of those ships for a young person who is willing to be flexible, put in the effort, and serve their country with honor.

# GLOSSARY

**administrative** Related to managing an organization.

**brutal** Very violent, cruel, or unpleasant.

**controversial** Causing disagreement or argument.

**collier** A bulk cargo ship that carries coal.

**convoy** A group of ships that travel together for safety.

**deck** Horizontal planking or plating that divides a ship into layers (never called a floor).

**deterrent** A means of preventing enemy attack by fear of retaliation.

**devastate** To totally destroy.

**escort** To accompany for protection.

**flagship** The vessel that carries the commander of a fleet of ships; has a flag to indicate the commander's rank.

**galley** The kitchen on a ship.

**hatch** An opening in a deck used for access.

**insurgent** A person who takes part in a rebellion against an established authority.

**integration** The policy of allowing people of all races, genders, and beliefs to serve together.

**knot** Nautical mile per hour.

**littoral** Of, relating to, or situated on the shore of the sea or a lake.

**mizzenmast** The third mast from the bow in a vessel.

**provision** To keep supplied with necessary goods.

**reconnaissance** An inspection of an area to gain information.

**tactical** Strategic.

**terrorism** The use of violence to support a political goal.

**U-boat** A submarine, although the term usually refers to a German submarine during World Wars I and II.

**unmanned aerial vehicle** An aircraft without a human pilot aboard; commonly called a "drone."

**vulnerable** Weak or at risk of being damaged.

# FOR MORE INFORMATION

## Military.com: Navy
133 Boston Post Road
Weston, MA 02493
Website: www.military.com/navy
Facebook, Instagram, and Twitter: @Militarydotcom
This website is a valuable resource for anyone who wants to learn more about the U.S. armed forces. Its page on the navy includes updated information on naval careers and pay grades.

## National Archives: Naval and Marine Records
700 Pennsylvania Avenue NW
Washington, DC 20408
Website: www.archives.gov/research/military/navy
Facebook: @usnationalarchives
Instagram and Twitter: @USNatArchives
Supported by the federal government, the U.S. Archives has detailed information about the nation's naval history, including primary sources and research guides for anyone interested in learning more about the navy.

## United Service Organizations (USO)
2111 Wilson Boulevard #1200
Arlington, VA 22201
Website: www.uso.org
Facebook and Instagram: @theUSO
Twitter: @the_USO
Founded in 1941, the USO is a charitable organization that helps soldiers adjust to civilian life after deployment. The USO is also known for providing live celebrity entertainment to troops while they are deployed.

## United States Naval Academy

121 Blake Road
Annapolis, MD 21402
Website: www.usna.edu/homepage.php
Facebook and Instagram: @USNavalAcademy
Twitter: @NavalAcademy
The U.S. Naval Academy is one of the most prestigious military colleges in the world, and its website offers information for aspiring sailors and students.

## United States Navy

1000 Navy Pentagon
Washington, DC 20350-1200
Website: www.navy.mil
Facebook, Instagram, and Twitter: @AmericasNavy
The official website of the U.S. Navy features information about joining the navy, what life is like as a sailor, and what career options are open to young recruits.

# FOR FURTHER READING

Baxter, Roberta. *Work in the Military*. San Diego, CA: BrightPoint Press, 2020.

Boothroyd, Jennifer. *Inside the US Navy*. Minneapolis, MN: Lerner Publications, 2018.

Borden, Louise. *Full Speed Ahead! America's First Admiral: David Glasgow Farragut*. New York, NY: Calkins Creek, 2021.

Conkling, Winifred, and Julia Kuo. *Heroism Begins with Her: Inspiring Stories of Bold, Brave, and Gutsy Women in the U.S. Military*. New York, NY: Harper, 2019.

Huddleston, Emma. *Life in the US Navy*. San Diego, CA: BrightPoint Press, 2021.

Hustad, Douglas. *U.S. Navy: Equipment and Vehicles*. Minneapolis, MN: Kids Core, 2022.

Mapua, Jeff. *Working with Tech in the Military*. New York, NY: Rosen Publishing, 2020.

Marx, Mandy R. *Amazing U.S. Navy Facts*. North Mankato, MN: Capstone Press, 2017.

Micklos, John. *SEAL Team Six: Battling Terrorism Worldwide*. North Mankato, MN: Capstone Press, 2017.

Mitchell, P. P. *Join the Navy*. New York, NY: Gareth Stevens Publishing, 2018.

Niver, Heather Moore. *Grace Hopper: Computer Scientist and Navy Admiral*. New York, NY: Enslow Publishing, 2019.

O'Brien, Cynthia. *Navy Careers*. New York, NY: Crabtree Publishing, 2021.

Perritano, John. *Take Out Bin Laden! Navy SEALs Hit the Most Wanted Man*. Broomall, PA: Mason Crest, 2019.

Phillips, Howard. *Inside the Navy SEALs*. New York, NY: PowerKids Press, 2022.

Zullo, Allan. *Heroes of Pearl Harbor*. New York, NY: Scholastic, 2019.

# INDEX

INDEX

frigates, 20, 51, 56, 57, 75

## G

Gravely, Samuel Lee, Jr., 64
Great White Fleet, 29, 50

## H

Haiti earthquake (2010), 52, 53
Hamilton, William, 8
Holland, John P., 24
Howard, Michelle, 64, 65, 67
Hull, Isaac, 12

## I

Indonesia tsunami (2004), 52, 53
intelligence officers, 84–86

## J

Jones, John Paul, 7–8
judge advocate generals, 84

## K

Katrina, Hurricane, 52, 53
Korean War, 30, 37–41, 42, 45, 61
Kuwait, Iraq invasion of, 45–46

## L

Langley, Sanuel P., 33
Lawrence, Wendy, 59
littoral combat ships (LCSs), 77

# ABOUT THE AUTHOR

Eric Ndikumana is a former collegiate long-distance runner who has been living in Rochester, New York, since 2018. In his free time, he enjoys spending time outdoors, exploring new trails and parks with friends and family.

# CREDITS

Designer: Michael Flynn; Editor: Siyavush Saidian